Steps I Will Follow in IIM

STEP 1 – TOPIC
Due:_____

STEP 2 – GOAL SETTING
Due:_____

STEP 3 – RESEARCH
Due:_____

STEP 4 – ORGANIZING
Due:_____

STEP 5 – GOAL EVALUATION
Due:_____

STEP 6 – PRODUCT
Due:_____

STEP 7 – PRESENTATION
Due:_____

As IIM Agents, we'll follow these steps to research success!

T0056271

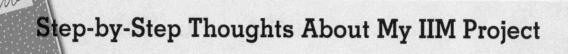

Step-by-Step Thoughts About My IIM Project

Name: _____

Unit: _____ My Topic: _____

Reflect on each step of IIM. Look back at your student booklet pages to help you remember.

STEP 1 Topic *Date completed:_____*

What I did well: _____

_____

What I will work on next time: _____

_____

Teacher comments: _____

_____

_____

STEP 2 Goal Setting *Date completed:_____*

What I did well: _____

_____

What I will work on next time: _____

_____

Teacher comments: _____

_____

_____

STEP 3 Research *Date completed:_____*

What I did well: _____

_____

What I will work on next time: _____

_____

Teacher comments: _____

_____

_____

Independent Investigation Method

Student Booklet

Hello, I'm Agent IIM. What's your name?

This book belongs to Agent

Name: _____

_____

By: _____

Grade: _____

Teacher: _____

Class IIM Unit

_____

My IIM Topic

_____

Date Started: _____

Date Finished: _____

STEP 4 Organizing *Date completed:_____*

What I did well: _____

_____

What I will work on next time: _____

_____

Teacher comments: _____

_____

STEP 5 Goal Evaluation *Date completed:_____*

What I did well: _____

_____

What I will work on next time: _____

_____

Teacher comments: _____

_____

STEP 6 Product *Date completed:_____*

What I did well: _____

_____

What I will work on next time: _____

_____

Teacher comments: _____

_____

STEP 7 Presentation *Date completed:_____*

What I did well: _____

_____

What I will work on next time: _____

_____

Teacher comments: _____

_____

Write ideas about your Topic on the Mind Map using what you already know and questions you have. Try grouping your ideas into categories.

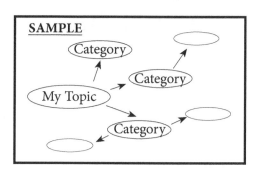

My Topic

My _____ Glossary
(Topic)

List the NEW words and their meanings that are key to the understanding of your topic.

_____   _____

                    _____

                    _____

_____   _____

                    _____

                    _____

_____   _____

                    _____

                    _____

_____   _____

                    _____

                    _____

_____   _____

                    _____

                    _____

_____   _____

                    _____

                    _____

My Research Goals

Notefact Goal: _____

Required Glossary Words: _____

Required Number of Resources: _____

Required Resource Types: _____

_____

_____

_____

_____

Resource Types

Book, magazine, Internet, TV show, letter, computer, interview, video/movie, poster, field trip...

My Topic: _____

Questions to Guide My Research
Teacher Question(s):

_____

_____

_____

_____

_____

_____

My Questions:

_____

_____

_____

_____

_____

_____

_____

Steps to Taking Notefacts

These are directions to help you take **notefacts** for your IIM using the *Notefacts* pages. If you follow these steps, you will be on the way to becoming a good researcher.

1. Each resource you use will have its own number. Write that number in the large magnifying glass and on all the small magnifying glasses on your *Notefacts* pages.

2. Record required information for your bibliography on the solid lines.

3. Now you're ready to take **notefacts**. Agent IIM calls them **notefacts** because they are short (notes) and true (facts).

4. **Notefacts** should be:

   - Written in your own words

   - Short but complete enough to make sense

   - Related to your goal setting questions

   - Written between the dotted lines —one **notefact** per space

   - Documented by page number

Don't be a plagiarist by stealing other authors' words

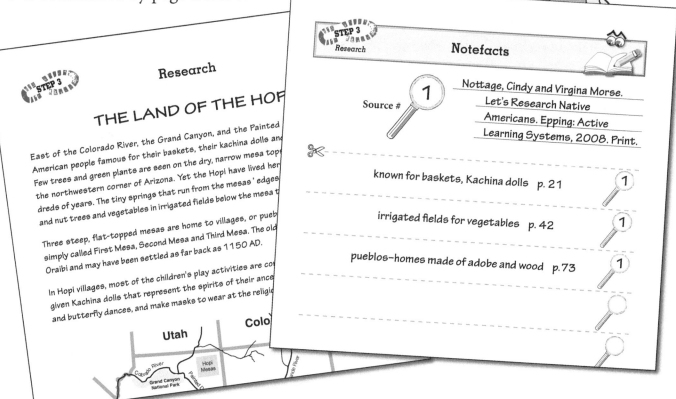

Use the MLA documentation style below in developing your:

1. *Working bibliography* – a record of all sources used in your research.
2. *Works cited* – a list of all sources that you cite in the text of your paper.

Print Sources

BOOK: Author(s). *Title*. City of publication: Publisher, Date. Medium.

> Parker, Derek and Julia Barker. *Atlas of the Supernatural*. New York: Prentice Hall, 2000. Print.

CHART, MAP, POSTER, PHOTOGRAPH: *Title*. City of publication: Publisher, Date. Medium.

> *The Solar System*. Palo Alto: Dale Seymour Publications, 2007. Poster.

ENCYCLOPEDIA AND REFERENCE BOOKS: "Title of article." *Title of book or publication*. Edition number. Year. Medium.

> "Crocodile." *Encyclopedia Americana*. 3rd edition. 2004. Print.

MAGAZINE: Author(s). "Title of article." *Name of magazine* Date: Page numbers. Medium.

> Satchell, Michael. "To Save the Sequoias." *US News and World Report* 7 Oct. 2006: 42-46. Print.

NEWSPAPER: Author. "Title of article." *Name of Newspaper* [City if not part of name] Date, edition (if listed): Page(s). Medium.

> Murphy, Sean. "It Floats." *Rockingham News* [Exeter, NH] 21 May 2009, late ed.: A12. Print.

PAMPHLET: Same style as book without author

Non-Print Sources

FIELD TRIP: Site. Location. Attending Group. Date.

> Longfellow-Evangeline State Commemorative Area. St. Martinville, LA. Grade 6, Maplewood Middle School. 13 March 2007.

INTERVIEW: Person interviewed. Type of interview (personal, telephone. . .). Date.

> Parsons, Mary. Telephone interview. 30 May 2008.

SOUND RECORDINGS: Artist. "Title of selection." Manufacturer, Date. Medium.

Kawamura, Masako. "Baratata-Batake." PWS Records, 1996. CD.

SPEAKER: Speaker. "Title." Sponsoring organization. Location. Date. Type of Presentation.

Landry, Bob. "Acadiens." Maplewood 6th Grade Team. Maplewood Middle School Auditorium, Sulphur, LA. 7 March 2009. Lecture.

TELEVISION OR RADIO PROGRAM: "Title of episode or segment." *Title of program*. Network. Call letters, City. Date(s). Medium.

"Secrets of Lost Empires." *Nova*. PBS. WGBH, Boston. 26 May 2007. Television.

VIDEO: *Title*. Director or producer. Distributor, Date. Medium.

Jurassic Park, The Lost World. Dir. Stephen Speilberg. Century Fox, 1995. DVD.

Electronic Sources

WEB PAGE: Author. "Title." Site sponsor or Internet site, Date of posting or latest update. Medium. Date of access. <Electronic address or URL> (if required).

Morse, Sarah. "Female Pedagogy." Morse Homepage, 25 May 2008. Web. 3 August 2009. <http://www.morsefamily.com>.

ENTIRE WEB SITE: Editor, author, or compiler name (if given). *Name of Site*. Date of posting or latest update. Name of sponsoring organization, Medium. Date of access. <Electronic address or URL> (if required).

House, Harold. *Building Green Homes*. 4 June 2008. Green Living, Web. 30 April 2009. <http://greenliving.org>.

NOTE 1: These samples are written as if you were doing your bibliography electronically. If you are handwriting the entries, underline the parts that are in italics.

NOTE 2: For more detailed directions and complete listings, see MLA Handbook for Writers of Research Papers *(Gibaldi 2009).*

*NOTE 3: You might want to use an electronic citation site. Be sure you have recorded all the necessary information while you are working on your notes. Two free sites are: Citation machine—*http://citationmachine.net *and Easy Bib—*www.easybib.com

Sources of Information

Notefacts

Notefacts

Notefacts

Moving From 1-4: ___Research___

(Step or Skill)

Name(s): _____

Topic: _____ Date: _____

For the Teacher: Create with class of assign criteria and indicators for quality work. If you decide to give a grade, use the total possible points to choose the range for letter grades.

1. Criterion: __Quantity of Notefacts_____

   Indicators: __At least_____ notefacts_____

   _____

   1 _____ 2 _____ 3 _____ 4

2. Criterion: __Quality of Notefacts_____

   Indicators: __Not copied, enough information, short, related to__

   __goal setting questions_____

   1 _____ 2 _____ 3 _____ 4

3. Criterion: __Number of resources_____

   Indicators: __At least_____ resources_____

   _____

   1 _____ 2 _____ 3 _____ 4

4. Criterion: __Types of resources_____

   Indicators: __At least_____ types_____

   _____

   1 _____ 2 _____ 3 _____ 4

Grading

A = _____   D = _____

B = _____   **Not**

C = _____   **Yet =** _____

   Final Grade = _____

Ratings

1 = Just Beginning   **3** = Made It

2 = Moving Up   **4** = Over the Top

Steps to Organizing

1. Think about categories as you read **all** your notefacts.
2. List categories at the bottom of this page.
3. Color the **handle** of each category lens a different color.
4. Write categories on *Organizing Notefacts* pages, one sheet for each category.

Notes About _____
(Your category name)

Your ← category color

5. Color code all your notefacts according to category colors. (Color handle only.)
6. Cut notefact strips.
7. Place color-coded notefact strips on each *Organizing Notefacts* page.
8. Rearrange the notefacts in an order that makes sense.
9. Check with your teacher.
10. Glue strips to pages.

Categories

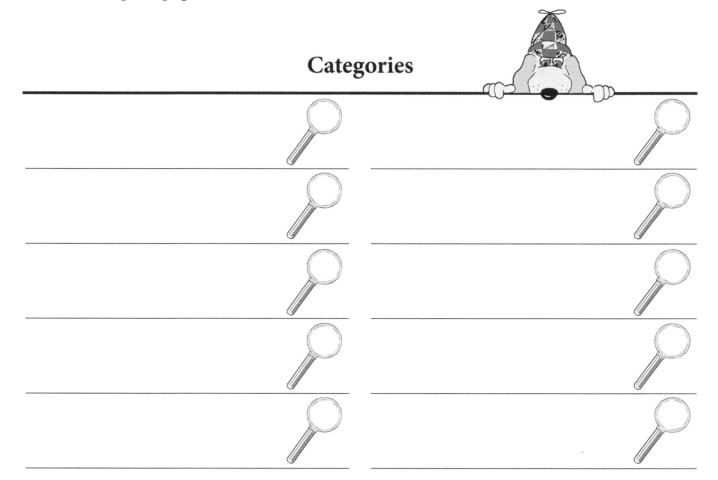

STEP 4
Organizing

My Organized Notefacts

Notes About_____

Attach your notefacts here

STEP 4
Organizing

My Organized Notefacts

Notes About_____

Attach your notefacts here

My Organized Notefacts

Notes About_____

Attach your notefacts here

STEP 4
Organizing

My Organized Notefacts

Notes About _____

Attach your notefacts here

My Organized Notefacts

Notes About _____

Attach your notefacts here

Evaluating My Research Goals
What I Learned

Notefact Goal: _____   Notefacts Written: _____

Required Number of Glossary Words: _____   Number of Glossary Words: _____

Required Number of Resources: _____   Number of Resources Used: _____

Required Resource Types: _____ _____ _____ _____

Goal Achieved (check):   ☐   ☐   ☐   ☐

Key Findings About My Topic

What are the most important findings and new ideas you would like to share with others when you reach Step 6 -Product?

1. _____

_____

_____

2. _____

_____

_____

3. _____

_____

_____

My Key Glossary Words: _____

_____

_____

My Future IIM Goals: _____

_____

Possible Goals

Number of note-facts, notefact quality, number of resources, resource types, goal setting questions, time management...

_____

_____

My New Ideas and Questions

Name: _____ Date: _____

My Topic: _____

Directions: Choose three of the following questions and write a short paragraph about each one as it relates to what you learned during your research.

1. Explain why this topic is important.
2. What surprised you?
3. What are the major issues around this topic?
4. How can you apply what you learned to your own life?
5. How has this study changed your thinking?
6. What are the questions you would still like to answer? Why?

Question _____

_____
_____
_____
_____
_____
_____

Question _____

_____
_____
_____
_____
_____
_____

Question_____

_____
_____
_____
_____
_____
_____

My Words at Work

Name(s): _____

Topic: _____   Date: _____

Write 3 words that are important to your study of _____

1. _____

2. _____

3. _____

Now, write 1 sentence using each word to show you understand its meaning.
Don't just use the definition.

Example: *No!* A <u>ball</u> is a round toy.
             Yes! My friend was bouncing his rubber <u>ball</u> on the playground

1. _____

_____

_____

2. _____

_____

_____

3. _____

_____

_____

4. _____

_____

_____

Choosing My Product

Your product must show what you've learned during IIM. Choose something:

- *that you enjoy* • *that will be interesting to your audience*
- *that is different from other products you've made*

Action: commercial, competition, dance, debate, demonstration, experiment, game, interview, lesson, performance, play, puppet show, scavenger hunt, speech, treasure hunt,

_____

Collection: collage, display, learning center, mini-museum, portfolio, scrapbook, terrarium,

_____

Model: diorama, invention, musical instrument, scale model, sculpture,

_____

Technology: animation, computer program, database, PowerPoint, photograph, radio/TV broadcast, recording, web page, Wiki blog, webinar, multimedia museum box,

_____

Visual Representation: bulletin board, cartoon, chart, concept map, costume, display board, family tree, flag, float, graph, map, mask, mobile, mural, needlework, painting, picture book, poster, project cube, puzzle, quilt, time line,

_____

Written Work: advertisement, book (ABC, biography, diary, fact, fantasy, flip book, journal, picture book, recipe book, science fiction, shape book), brochure, crossword puzzle, dictionary, fact cards, letter, magazine, news report, poetry, riddle, song, travel log, word search,

Remember!
- Be sure your product shares what you've learned during your research
- Plan carefully
- Leave enough time to make a quality product
- Proofread your work

_____

My Audience Will Be:

_____

My Product Plan

Product: _____

List the steps you will follow in making your product:

_____   _____

_____   _____

_____   _____

List the materials you will need:

_____   _____

_____   _____

_____   _____

What problem(s) might keep you from completing your product?

_____   _____

_____   _____

Use this space (or the back of the page) to draw a diagram of your product.

Be sure to label your diagram!

Planning My Presentation

Product: _____

Audience: _____

Method of Presentation: *(Describe and list steps)*

_____

_____

_____

_____

Materials I Will Need:

☐ Notecards

☐ Visual Aids—list:

☐ Handout—attach copy

☐ Equipment—list:

_____   _____

_____   _____

_____   _____

 ## Last Chance Check!

1. Practice your presentation.
2. Evaluate both your product and presentation.
3. Circle what you have done well.
4. Improve those things that aren't circled.

My Product:

Teaches something I've learned

Uses correct spelling and grammar

Is a creative way to share information

My Presentation:

Teaches something I've learned

Is clear and well organized

Uses quality speaking voice: slow, clear, and loud

Is interesting to audience

How High Can I Go? __Presentation__

(Step or Skill)

Name(s): _____

Topic: _____ Date: _____

Name of Peer Evaluator: _____

For the Teacher: Create with class or assign criteria for quality work. If you decide to give a grade, use the total possible points to choose the range for letter grades.

CRITERIA	STUDENT OR PEER	TEACHER	COMMENT
Shows knowledge of topic			
Organized			
Interesting			
Quality visuals			
Uses imagination & creativity			
Good voice tone			
Makes eye contact			
TOTAL			

Grading

A = _____ D = _____

B = _____ Not

C = _____ Yet = _____

Final Grade = _____

Ratings

1 = Just Beginning **3** = Made It

2 = Moving Up **4** = Over the Top